Pirate TALES

PATHFINDER EDITION

By Francis Downey and Sara Lorimer

CONTENTS

Pirate King

Scientists Search for the Real Blackbeard

By Francis Downey

SCIENTISTS HAVE FOUND a sunken treasure off the North Carolina coast. It's not a pirate's treasure, but it may be an old pirate ship.

Archaeologists, scientists who study the past, think they have found Blackbeard's ship. He may be the most famous pirate of all. His ship, the *Queen Anne's Revenge*, sank in 1718. Since then, the ship has been lost at sea and to history.

Now that's changing. So far, a bell, several cannons, and part of the ship's hull, or body, have been brought to the surface. The objects are helping scientists learn about life on a pirate ship. Let's sail with Blackbeard and his **crew** to see what their lives were like.

BLACKBEARD KNEW how to make a first impression. A large black beard covered his face. He may have stuck lit candles under his hat. Witnesses say flames leapt from his face and smoke circled his head. It looked like he was on fire.

Sea Sagas

Amazing stories about Blackbeard's pirate adventures followed him wherever he went. Some were true, but many were made up. Despite these tales, little is known about him.

Historians don't even know Blackbeard's real name, which isn't surprising. Many pirates made up their names. They didn't want anyone to know who they really were.

All the records from Blackbeard's time call him either Blackbeard or Edward Teach. His name, however, was spelled in different ways. Some list him as Thatch, Thack, or Thatche.

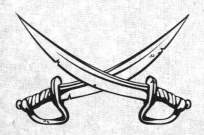

Finding Blackbeard

Teach's Teacher

Little is known about Blackbeard before he became a pirate. No one really even knows where he was born. Most say he was born in England, but some say he was born in America.

Wherever he was born, we think we know where he was in 1716. At that time, Blackbeard lived on a small island called New Providence. Blackbeard met Captain Benjamin Hornigold, a pirate **captain**, on the island.

Blackbeard may have joined Hornigold's crew. If so, they set out for adventure. Blackbeard learned all he could from his teacher. He soon became such a good pirate that Hornigold gave Blackbeard a ship. The two ships sailed together, the pirate captains plundering every ship they found.

Pirate Plunder

Late the following year, Blackbeard spotted a ship in the distance and quickly barked orders. His crew sprang into action. They tugged on the rigging, or ropes, they tacked the sails, and they pushed the tiller. The ship turned and sped toward the new target.

The ship's crew got ready for a fight. Most important, they hoisted the pirate flag. Pirates used many different flags. That's because they made their own. The flags were usually black. The most famous, called the Jolly Roger, had a skull and crossbones on it.

As soon as the pirates neared the ship, they fired at it. A couple of cannonballs smashed through its hull. The crew was so scared that they quickly **surrendered**. The ship and its crew and cargo were now pirate plunder.

Blackbeard took the captured ship, which he renamed *Queen Anne's Revenge*, after a queen of England. Blackbeard was now the captain of several pirate ships.

Unwanted Guests. *Smoke rises from a damaged ship as pirates prepare to come on board.*

A Pirate's Life

It wasn't easy being a pirate captain. True, captains were in charge of their ships, but they were not dictators. Their crews elected them. Captains had to be brave. They also had to be smart and ruthless. If they weren't, their crews would replace them.

Life for a pirate crew wasn't easy either. They lived and worked on a ship's deck. Oftentimes, they didn't have enough food or water. They rarely bathed or changed clothes. Many got sick. Fights broke out.

Pirates had to follow the pirate code. If they broke a rule, punishments were harsh. Pirates never walked the plank. That is just a myth. However, some were tied, tossed into the water, and dragged behind the ship.

Crew members came from a variety of countries and spoke different languages. Still, they had some things in common. They all wanted to get rich, and they were all criminals.

Port of Call

Pirate attacks weren't always about money. In his most famous adventure in 1718, Blackbeard sailed to the port city of Charleston, South Carolina. He took several prisoners and threatened to kill them unless the city's citizens gave him medicine. Fearing the worst, the citizens soon handed over the medicine.

In less than two years, Blackbeard had blockaded a town and captured more than 50 ships. Then Blackbeard decided he no longer wanted to be a pirate. He sank his ship off North Carolina. The governor of North Carolina then **pardoned** him for his crimes.

Blackbeard now led the life of a gentleman. He may have lived in a large house. He dined with the governor of North Carolina and married the daughter of a wealthy farmer. Many people respected him.

A Pirate's End

Yet a quiet life wasn't what Blackbeard really wanted. He soon got together with some of his old crew and went on pirate raids again.

These new plundering pirate raids didn't last for very long. Pirates made enemies—lots of enemies.

The governor of Virginia was one of Blackbeard's enemies. He sent a crew to kill Blackbeard. They found him on a ship with his old pirate crew. Outnumbered, Blackbeard was no match for his attackers. He soon joined many other pirates at the bottom of the ocean in Davy Jones's locker.

Fact or Fiction? *Did Blackbeard (standing in center) really have his men bury treasure? No one knows.*

The career of a pirate was short. Most only lasted at sea for two or three years. Blackbeard was no exception. Yet while the names of most pirates are now lost at sea, Blackbeard's legend lives on. Today, many people think of him and other pirates as heroes. At the time, most sailors feared them. Pirates were the most dreaded outlaws of their time.

Wordwise

captain: the person in charge of a ship

crew: the people who work on a ship

pardon: let go without punishment

surrender: to stop fighting

BRINGING UP PIRATE BOUNTY

ON THE NIGHT of April 26, 1717, a ship ran into a violent storm off the coast of Cape Cod, Massachusetts. That ship was called the *Whydah Galley*. The ship hit a sandbar and sank. All but two members of the ship's crew went down with the ship.

The *Whydah Galley* was lost on the ocean floor for 267 years. Then in July 1984, archaeologists discovered its location. Since then, archaeologists have found thousands of artifacts from the wreck.

Archaeologists preserve and study artifacts to learn what life was like aboard the ship. But how exactly do you study artifacts at the bottom of the ocean?

That's where underwater archaeology comes in. Underwater archaeologists study ships and other artifacts that are buried under water.

Underwater archaeologists face many challenges. The biggest one is breathing! To breathe under water, they must wear heavy air tanks. This makes their work hard and show. Read on to see what other challenges they face!

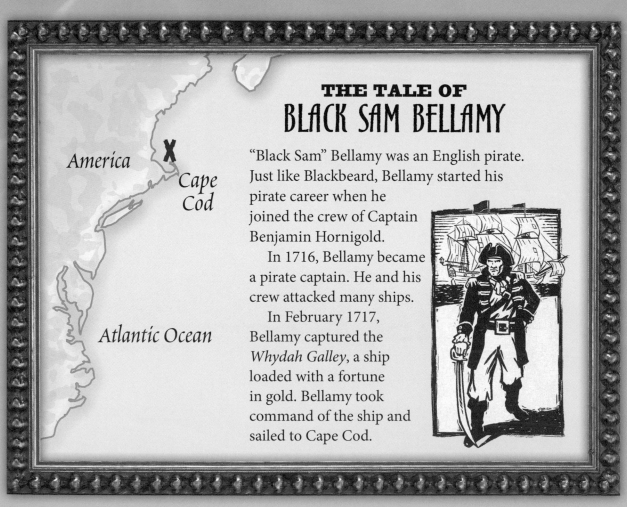

America

X

Cape Cod

Atlantic Ocean

THE TALE OF
BLACK SAM BELLAMY

"Black Sam" Bellamy was an English pirate. Just like Blackbeard, Bellamy started his pirate career when he joined the crew of Captain Benjamin Hornigold.

In 1716, Bellamy became a pirate captain. He and his crew attacked many ships.

In February 1717, Bellamy captured the *Whydah Galley*, a ship loaded with a fortune in gold. Bellamy took command of the ship and sailed to Cape Cod.

These gold coins and jewelry are treasures from the Whydah.

How do archaeologists locate artifacts?
Here an archaeologist uses a light and a metal detector (right) to find small items from the *Whydah*, such as coins and pieces of jewelry.

How do archaeologists uncover artifacts?
They carefully brush sand away as they uncover artifacts. Here an archaeologist discovers part of the *Whydah's* hull, or body.

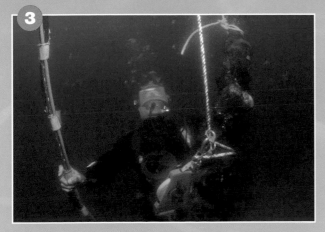

How do archaeologists bring artifacts up from the water? They attach ropes and airbags. As the bags floats upward, they lift the item up, too. Here an archaeologist watches a small cannon from the *Whydah* rise to the surface.

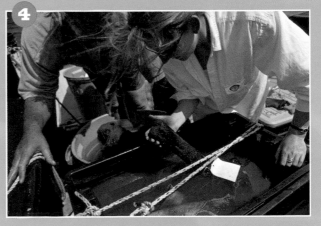

How do archaeologists protect artifacts?
They store them in buckets of water. This keeps items from drying out. Here an archaeologist examines a piece of wood from the *Whydah*.

Girl Pirates

By Sara Lorimer

For as long as there have been pirates, some of those pirates have been girls and women. Piracy offered women freedoms that were denied them on land. Plus there was no household to run, no family to support, no chamber pots to empty. At sea, a woman kept her own hours and spent them drinking, gambling, sailing, eating, and plundering. Some pirate women followed their boyfriends into piracy. Others tried it out after spending time in the military (disguised as men). Still others carried out a family tradition.

Mary Read and Anne Bonney

REIGN OF TERROR: THE CARIBBEAN, EARLY 1700S

X After Mary Read's husband died, she needed money. So she signed up as a sailor on a merchant ship sailing to the West Indies. When the ship reached the Caribbean, English pirates took it over. They gave Mary a choice: Join up or be killed. Mary officially turned pirate.

Mary soon had a chance to show off her dueling skills. Fearing that her boyfriend on the ship would be killed in a duel, Mary picked a fight with the challenger and scheduled a duel herself—two hours before her beau's. Mary defeated the other pirate without suffering a single scratch.

Mary met Anne Bonney, who ran away to sea with a flashy pirate named Calico Jack, when both women ended up on Jack's ship. Together they attacked other boats, mostly stealing small items like fishing gear and food. Despite the minor nature of their plundering, the English authorities issued a proclamation declaring Jack and the gals "Enemies to the Crown of Great Britain."

Fierce Fighter *Mary Read wins a duel against a male opponent.*

Rachel Wall

REIGN OF TERROR: NEW ENGLAND COAST, LATE 1700S

X Rachel Wall sailed along the coast of Maine with her husband, George, and their crew. After storms they'd moor their ship and raise a distress flag. When passersby responded to Rachel's screams for help, they were attacked for their trouble. In two summers of piracy, Rachel and George killed 24 men, maybe more—and raked in $6,000 cash, plus an unknown amount of valuable goods. They later sold their loot, by pretending that they found it washed up on a beach.

Cheng I Sao

REIGN OF TERROR: SOUTH CHINA SEA, 1801–1810

X The greatest pirate of all time (by the numbers, anyway) was Cheng I Sao, who ruled a terrifying fleet of 2,000 ships in the South China Sea. Cheng I Sao, sometimes called Madame Cheng, turned to crime when she married a famous pirate. More than 80,000 pirates—men, women, and even children—did Madame Cheng's bidding. They seized loot in all sorts of ways—selling "protection" from pirate attacks, raiding ships, and kidnapping. Madame Cheng paid her pirates cash for the prizes they brought back from their assaults.

CRIME DOESN'T PAY, even on the high seas—or does it? Mary Read and Anne Bonney were captured in 1720. Mary died of fever while she was in prison; what happened to Anne is a mystery. Eventually the law caught up with Rachel Wall, too. In 1789, she made history when she was the last woman to be executed in Massachusetts. Government attempts to stop Madame Cheng, however, all met with failure. Rumor has it that after she retired from piracy, she embarked on a second career as a smuggler. She died peacefully at age 69.

Pirate Treasure

Answer these question to discover your own pirate bounty.

1 Why is finding Blackbeard's ship important?

2 How did Blackbeard become a pirate? List the events in order.

3 Describe Blackbeard's life during retirement. Why did he become a pirate again?

4 What makes underwater archaeology difficult?

5 Why did some women become pirates? What happened to pirates—both men and women?